Nothing Is Random

Cassidy Cornblatt

ISBN-13: 978-1495264795
ISBN-10: 1495264793

To Tekla Cobb,

for introducing me to these ideas.

Acknowledgements

I would like to thank the following people for their contributions: Colin Renick, Derek Wagner, Philip Cornblatt, Natasha Cornblatt, and Frank Magalhães.

Table of Contents

Introduction

Nothing is random. Everything that has ever happened was guaranteed to happen. Free will is just a necessary illusion.

My friend introduced me to this idea nearly a year ago, and it is still messing with my mind to this day. At first I was skeptical, like most people. As a science major, randomness seems incredibly important. The basis of evolution is random mutations. How can we understand the world without randomness? Is everything preplanned? Do we even have any control over our own futures? I will delve into these issues later. For now, I have to convince you that I am not completely crazy.

Games of Chance

So at this point, you're probably thinking to yourself, "What is this guy talking about? Life is full of random occurrences." And on the surface, at least, you would be right. However, if you really think about seemingly random things, you will begin to see that they are not truly random at all.

Let's start simple – with a coin flip. Everybody knows that when you flip a coin, the chance to get heads is approximately 50% (usually ±1% in studies). So that means that when you flip a coin, getting either heads or tails is completely random, right? Wrong. The outcome of the flip depends on a variety of factors: the side the coin started on, the weight balance between the two sides, the speed at which the coin was flipped, the angle at which the coin was flipped, air resistance, gravity, and whatever the coin lands on (which will add friction into the mix). If you were to flip a coin in exactly the same way every time, you would get the exact same result. So if you flipped a coin and got heads, what is the chance that this would have happened? 50%? No, 100%. You were guaranteed to get heads based on how you flipped the coin.

Now you're starting to get the idea, but coin flips are too easy. There are only two possible outcomes (well three if you get it to land on its edge). Let's take a look at something a bit more complicated – rolling a six-sided die. So you roll a die and get a six. There was only a 1/6 chance of rolling that. Feeling lucky? You shouldn't be. You were guaranteed to roll that six based on how you tossed the die onto the table. The outcome depended on the position the die was held in your hand, the angle and speed with which it left your hand, and the friction of the table. If you could roll it exactly as you did before, you would again roll a six. This is very difficult for a human to accomplish, but it brings to mind a scene from the cancelled show *Terminator: The Sarah Connor Chronicles* in which a reprogrammed terminator is taught to play Dungeons & Dragons. The robot successively rolls 20s on a twenty-sided die without fail once it realizes that 20 is a good number to roll in the game. Though a fictional show, it demonstrated that a robot could roll a die to achieve a desired outcome every time. The outcome of the roll is not random.

This is still a fairly simple example, however. In an attempt to come up with something that seems much more random and harder to explain, you suggest shuffling cards. I'll do you one better. You shuffle a deck of cards and cut the deck, and then you take the top card. It's a seven of clubs. What is the probability that this happened? Common sense would dictate 1/52. Common sense would be wrong. Again, there was a 100% chance that this happened because it did happen. "How?" you ask. "That doesn't seem possible."

I'll explain. The cards all had original locations in the deck. The deck was split near the middle to shuffle the cards. The person who split the deck will tend to split it in a similar place each time. When the cards were shuffled, they were simply moved around depending on their placement relative to the others, the friction of card against card, and the bending of the cards. Then the deck was cut in the same manner as it was split before. The card that ended up on top was always going to end up on top if the deck was shuffled and cut in that exact manner.

Let's take a look at something that seems really random – the lottery. Depending on which lottery you're playing, the odds for winning vary. However, they are usually very low, so that person who won $200,000,000 must have been really lucky, right? By now you know where I'm going with this. That person was guaranteed to win. Here we start getting into more complicated matters. This is not just about a supposedly random machine not being random; it is also about a person's life leading to this moment.

I'll start with the lottery machine. There are many different types of lotteries, but I am going to focus on the ones with the Ping-Pong-like balls. Before the balls leave the machine, they are mixed around with either air or paddles. Their final location in the machine determines which ball is chosen. The balls reach this location due to contact with other balls and with the air or paddles. The continual mixing is supposed to ensure randomness, but the balls that are chosen are completely determined by their interactions with the other balls and parts of the machine. If this could be replicated exactly, the machine would choose the same balls. Well, this seems like sort of a stretch, but the point is that everything is determined by previous occurrences.

Now let's discuss the person buying the ticket. They had to be at the right place at the right time to buy that particular winning ticket. That seems like luck, but it is actually a result of previous things happening in that person's life. What led that person to that store? This could get quite detailed, so I'm going to give the person a name to make it easier to follow. Let's call the person Ron. Maybe Ron was filling up gas before heading home from a family vacation. His daughter was hungry, so at his wife's urgings, he went into the store to get a bag of chips. While he was in there, he glanced at the TV, and a news story about a flood caught his attention. He stood with the bag of chips and watched for a moment. Meanwhile, a woman walked by him to the register. Ron looked away from the TV and got in line behind her. The woman, who seemed to be a local, talked to the clerk, who told her that the lottery had reached a record high. She decided to buy a ticket and then left. Ron paid for the bag of chips and started to leave, but then he happened to glance down at his torn jeans on the way out. Thinking that he could really use some money to buy new clothes, he turned back around. "I think I'll take a lottery ticket," he said. When he got home late that night, he found out that he had won $200,000,000.

"Wow, what luck!" you say, but luck really had nothing to do with it. A long series of causes resulted in Ron's big win. He was out of town on vacation, his daughter was hungry, his wife made him go into the store, the TV played a story that got his attention, a woman got before him in line, the clerk told the woman about the lottery, and the man was wearing his torn pair of jeans. All of these things led to Ron buying the winning ticket. If one of these things had not happened, Ron wouldn't have gotten a lottery ticket, or he wouldn't have gotten the winning lottery ticket. But all of these things did happen, and they were guaranteed to happen. Everything led up to this.

Causes and Effects

Here's an easier way to think about it. Everything in life follows a simple cause and effect system. When certain things happen, they result in a particular outcome. For example, you're hungry and see a restaurant while you're driving, so you stop to get food. That's easy enough to understand. Now let's make it a bit more complex. Each cause is actually an effect of previous causes. If we go back to the previous example, you are hungry because you woke up late, and you are driving to get to work. You decide to stop because the restaurant is on your way, and you don't plan to stay for long. These causes for your current situation can be traced back even further. You woke up late because you stayed up the night before watching a TV show on Netflix. You were watching that show because your friend recommended it. Your friend recommended it because he enjoyed it. He watched it because he saw a favorable review online. We could take this back further and further indefinitely. So now you can see that you were guaranteed to stop at that restaurant to get food.

Let's look at another example. It is a beautiful day, and you are driving down the highway. You are enjoying your music when you suddenly hear sirens behind you. You look in your rearview mirror and see a police officer. "Darn," you say, "if only I had gotten back over into the right-hand lane after I passed that tractor-trailer." Well don't bother thinking about what you could have done to avoid this because this was guaranteed to happen. We can trace the causes again. You were pulled over because you were speeding and the police officer was there. You were speeding because it was a nice day, the road was relatively open, and you were in the left-hand lane. It was a nice day because there was a high pressure system over the area. The road was relatively open because it was the middle of the day on Tuesday. You were in the left-hand lane because you had just passed a tractor-trailer and you wanted to pass another slow vehicle you saw up ahead. There was a high pressure system because a front had moved through the day before. You were driving in the middle of the day on Tuesday because you wanted to avoid traffic. You passed the tractor-trailer because it was going below the speed limit. The police officer was there to pull you over because he was patrolling the road. He was patrolling the road because there had been issues with speeders there before and the police station needed money. There had been issues with speeders before because the road was flat and there didn't seem to be too many people who used it regularly. The police station needed money because their budget had been cut by the government. All of these things could be traced back further and further until you come to the conclusion that you were guaranteed to get pulled over for speeding on that road at that time.

These series of causes and effects create a web where every action and occurrence influences one another to determine the future. Actually, it is more like a cone web, since everything can be traced back to some point far in the past. You can visualize it like this:

Cone Web

Side View   Front View

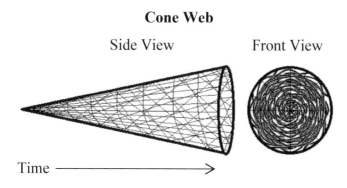

Time ————————————————→

      This shows the interactions of causes and effects over time. As time goes on, there are more and more events that can interact with each other, causing the cone's diameter to increase. If the cone is looked at from the front, the varying spirals and lines of causes and effects can be seen originating from the center and interacting along the way to the present. This model suggests that if all of these causes and effects were traced back far enough, they would coincide at a starting point. There are currently two main ideas about what this starting point could be: the Big Bang theory and religion (and sometimes a combination of both). In basic terms, the Big Bang theory states that at one instant in time, everything was contained in a single point, and then suddenly the Universe expanded out of this point and was born. This is what mathematic and scientific models point to as the beginning, though there are some dissenters in the scientific community. The other well-known option lies with religion. I say religion rather than God because depending on the religion, there are a variety of creation stories. What all of these religions have in common is that they do indeed have a creation story to explain where everything came from. In Christianity, Judaism, and Islam, God created the Universe, the Earth, and mankind. This may differ in other religions, but the important point is that every religion attempts to explain how everything began. In doing so, they admit that there must be a reason for everything to be as it is today. In this, science and faith agree.

Something I hear all the time is "Everything happens for a reason." But is this actually true? We have established that everything happens due to reasons. There are reasons for why everything is the way it is in the present. However, this saying suggests that everything that happens leads to something in particular in the future. No one can deny that everything leads to the future, but does everything lead to some mystical, significant event in the future? That is ridiculous. As the cone web idea shows, everything is not leading to a point in the future but instead is leading to an ever-expanding, more and more intricate future. What if you were to look at the strand of a single person's life in the cone web? Would it lead to some great event? Well sure, it would contain all of the big events in the person's life, but the only thing it would lead to is death. Everything does not happen for a reason. Everything happens because of reasons. Life is simply life, one segment along the cone web.

So is everything predetermined by cause and effect? How can nothing be random when you hear so much about probability and chance?

<u>Perceived Uncertainty</u>

I am going to explain where all of this random talk comes from. As a naturally curious species, we humans are very interested in what the future might bring. However, even though the future is already determined by the present and the past, we still cannot tell with certainty what is going to happen. All we can hope to do is to predict it with some degree of accuracy. This is where probability comes in.

Let's look back at an earlier example. You flip a coin. While the coin is in the air, neither you nor anyone else knows what it will land on. The coin is going to land on either heads or tails, and this outcome has already been determined before it happens. However, you do not know what the outcome will be, so you say there is a 50-50 chance of heads or tails. You guess tails, and to your delight, the coin lands on tails. Were you lucky? No, the coin was guaranteed to land on tails. Then you were lucky to guess the guaranteed outcome, right? Again no, because you had a reason to say tails, whether because you said heads last time or you think the coin favors tails. Well then at least you were lucky that the long series of causes and effects since the beginning of time allowed you to guess the right outcome this particular time, correct? Maybe, that gets more complicated, but since you were guaranteed to guess tails and the coin was guaranteed to land on tails, there's not really a whole lot of luck there.

Now we'll discuss the lottery again. We already established earlier that the lottery winner is predetermined, but nobody knows beforehand who it is going to be. For this reason, we calculate the probability that someone is going to be a winner. When it comes to the lottery, this is always a very low probability, such as 1 in 3 million, which makes us feel like the lottery is very random. What this really means is that we are very unsure who the winner is going to be.

This perceived uncertainty is also present with the weather. Meteorologists predict the weather by looking at causes and effects at the atmospheric level. They then devise a best guess of what they believe the weather is going to be in the future. The weather is already determined, but we do not know with complete certainty what it is going to be. We can only say that there will be a 70% chance of rain next Thursday because to us, the future is unknown.

But should our uncertainty about the future cause us to label predetermined events as random? I think not. By now, hopefully you have come to understand my point. Nothing is random. There are reasons behind everything. This is known as determinism. If you are still skeptical, think up a real counterexample and let me know. I would very much like to hear it.

So if this is all true, what does it mean? What are the implications?

Before we move on, I would like to discuss the rationales of the dissenters to this idea.

Radiation, Cats, and Parallel Universes

Despite the sense determinism makes, there are some people who disagree with it. Their main arguments center around two things: radioactive decay and quantum mechanics. The macroscopic world has been fairly conclusively proven to not be random, so in order to undermine this, people look at much smaller issues. They figure that if the things that make everything work are random, then everything is not predetermined.

I'll start with radioactive decay. There are certain elements that are radioactive, for example carbon-14 and uranium. This means that they are unstable and undergo a process of decay, the most commonly discussed being alpha, beta, and gamma. I'm not going to go into what each of these mean here because it is not important to the discussion at hand. What is important is that after a certain period of time, these elements will expel a particle or energy to reach a more stable state. Measuring carbon-14 decay is used to date organic materials, meaning plant and animal remains such as wood and bones. When we have a large quantity of radioactive material, we can calculate the decay rate and predict how it will decay. However, when we only have a single atom, we cannot predict when it will decay. It seems to decay randomly because we have not figured out a method for determining exactly when it will decay. But do not be fooled, this is not random; it is a simple case of perceived uncertainty. The atom is going to decay at a particular, predetermined time probably based on how unstable the atom is. If we were to record when such an atom decayed and then somehow go back in time, the atom would again decay at the exact same moment. It only seems random because we do not know when it will happen ahead of time.

Now we'll move on to the more confusing topic: quantum mechanics. This is the study of quanta, which are the most basic and smallest amounts of physical entities. The problem with studying such tiny things is that it is very hard to gather data on them. In fact, we have an incredibly difficult time just gathering data on their present state. In order to do so, we have to interact with the quanta and measure the reactions. This has provided some interesting results. Basically matter exists as both a particle and a wave. This causes the quanta to respond differently at times for seemingly no reason, giving rise to a variety of theories. These are often thought experiments since we cannot prove these in reality at least at the moment. The two big theories are the Copenhagen Interpretation and the Many-Worlds Interpretation.

The Copenhagen Interpretation states that all possibilities exist at once until something is observed, at which time one option is chosen randomly. The example typically used with this is the thought experiment of Schrödinger's Cat. For anyone who doesn't know what that is, it's basically this: a cat is placed in a box for an hour with a radioactive substance and a Geiger counter rigged so that if decay is measured, a hammer will smash a bottle of acid, killing the cat. Since we as outside observers do not know if the substance has decayed, we do not know if the cat is alive or dead until the hour is up. This apparently makes the cat theoretically both alive and dead at the same time until the box is opened. But in actuality this is another case of perceived uncertainty. The Copenhagen Interpretation is basically a refusal to believe that we cannot at this moment discern the state of a quantum. The cat in the box is either alive or dead. It cannot be both. If we could make a window in the box, we could see whether the cat was living. In the same way, if we could measure the current state of a quantum, we wouldn't need theories to make us feel better about not being able to gather this data.

The Many-Worlds Interpretation has the same problem. The idea behind this interpretation is that when there are two possibilities, the Universe splits into two to accommodate both. For example, in the cat situation described above, the cat lives in one universe and dies in a parallel universe. So rather than the cat being alive and dead at the same time in one universe, it is alive and dead at the same time in parallel universes. This is meant to make more sense in that the cat can only be either living or dead in each universe but is still both overall in all the universes. As I stated in the first sentence of this paragraph, the first issue with this idea is the perceived uncertainty factor again; still we are making excuses for not having figured out a way to get good data on quanta. There is another large problem with this interpretation as well: if we are guaranteed to make a particular choice and nothing is random, the Universe would never split. There cannot be parallel universes in this way because everything is guaranteed to happen the way it is. There are never multiple possibilities, only one path that the Universe can take.

Now that we have looked at and refuted the main evidence people use to reject the idea that nothing is random, we can move on to implications.

<u>Free Will</u>

So let's begin with a difficult but important topic: free will. This is the concept that we as individuals have conscious control over our own destinies and can make our own choices. This is an issue that is very personal for people. However, this is something we must discuss in our study of randomness. Let's think about it. If nothing is random and the present is guaranteed due to causes and effects in the past, can there realistically be free will? Some argue that though the past and present are set in stone, the future can be altered through our choices, but I cannot see how that is possible.

Is there such a thing as a choice? It may depend on how the word "choice" is defined. I would define choice as a point at which multiple options could realistically be chosen, leading to alternate futures. With this definition, I do not think choices really exist. There are no points at which multiple options can realistically be chosen. The decision someone makes is guaranteed based on previous factors. There are no other real options. If that person was to be reinserted in the past in the same exact situation again, they would make the exact same decision. There is a definition that allows choice, but it is a shallow imitation. This definition is the following: choice is a situation in which there seems to an uninformed onlooker to be a potential diverging of future paths. Choice exists with this definition, but only as an illusion of itself.

Let's look at some examples. Say you are faced with a difficult decision: you can either get an internship over the summer or go on a family vacation abroad. After much thought, eventually you choose to take the internship, but was this really a choice you made of your own free will? Your decision was decided by pre-existing factors. The internship is paid, so not only would it look good on your résumé, it would also give you spending money. It also concerns a subject that interests you. A family vacation abroad is enticing because you could see new locales and explore the world, but perhaps you would rather go with friends. If possible, you would like to squeeze both into your summer, but unfortunately, this is not possible. You choose the internship based on the factors we discussed.

Here's a more commonplace example: you are at a restaurant, and you have to decide on a meal. You can choose anything on the menu, right? Not exactly, your choice is already made for you. Again, this is due to pre-existing factors. Perhaps you have a fondness for chicken, or you had pasta the night before and want something different. Maybe the dinner selection simply catches your eye as you turn the page based on its placement or formatting. You also may not want to order the same thing as the others at your table, or maybe you want to share. Perhaps you find the waitress or waiter attractive, and so you pay extra attention as they tell you the specials. There are innumerable factors at play behind your decision, but regardless, your decision is already made. You cannot make a different decision given the current circumstances.

Though we have established that free will does not exist, this does not mean it is not important. Many people hold the concept very dear to their hearts. It has been shown that reducing a person's belief in their free will often leads to aggression and hostile behavior. People want to feel that they have control over their lives, although it can also be comforting to know that the present could not have been changed by a different choice in the past.

Crime

If nothing is random, one problem that arises is crime. Obviously crimes occur, but the issue is that people had no choice in committing them. If a person's life led to them committing a crime, then they were guaranteed to commit it and had no free will. Can you convict someone for a crime if they had no choice in the matter?

If someone forced you to commit a crime, should you be charged for it? You would rather the person who forced you to do it be charged. This is not possible if life forced you to commit a crime. You cannot charge life. So the question remains: are you accountable for your actions? I believe this is the basis of the insanity defense. The idea is that if people are insane, then they do not have control of their actions, so they cannot be charged with a crime. However, if no one has control of their actions, no one would be charged with a crime. This simply does not make sense.

I believe that people still have to be charged with crimes they commit. If they commit a crime, they are breaking a law, regardless of whether or not they had a choice. We cannot let people get away with crimes just because they had reasons for committing them. We have laws, and these laws influence our actions. Therefore it is only fair to follow through with the punishment for breaking these laws.

Think about it this way. If people were not punished for breaking the law, then this would cause them to break the law again since there were no consequences. The cause and effect system is still at play. Consequences cannot be removed simply because people have reasons for their actions. It is the crimes themselves that have consequences, not the reason why they were committed, though the reason may be taken into account in a courtroom. A lack of free will should not be used as an excuse; instead it should be taken as an observation.

Entropy

Now let's move on to a concept that is fundamentally important to science: entropy. I was always taught that entropy is a measure of disorder, otherwise known as randomness or the lack of organization in a system. I found out recently that it is more specifically a measure of energy dispersal. The second law of thermodynamics states that the entropy of a system always tends to increase if it is not hindered from doing so. Simple examples of this are hot pans cooling in the air and food dye mixing with water without stirring.

This concept is quite significant across disciplines. In physics, this helps explain the expansion of the Universe. In chemistry, entropy, in combination with enthalpy (total energy of a system) and temperature, dictates whether a reaction will occur.

$$\Delta G \quad = \quad \Delta H \quad - \quad T \quad \quad \Delta S$$

| Gibbs free energy | Enthalpy | Temperature | Entropy |

The above equation means that if entropy is increasing and energy is released (or one overcomes a lack of the other), then a reaction will be spontaneous at a particular temperature. This is another example of how the Universe is not random. Chemical reactions determine much of what we experience and observe in the world. Whether or not these reactions progress is determined by the entropy, enthalpy, and temperature of the reactions. Keep in mind, however, that the rate of reactions is a different story, though there are equations that can calculate that as well.

Hopefully you now have a basic understanding of entropy if you did not already. I will now discuss how what I was taught is incorrect. Entropy cannot be a measure of disorder if there is no such thing as disorder. Disorder implies randomness. There cannot be disorder if everything is ordered by cause and effect to seem like a state of disorder. A common example teachers use to introduce entropy is a teenager's bedroom. The once clean room becomes more disordered over time, and energy is required to re-order it. But the room does not really become disordered; it just becomes ordered in a different way. Clothes might pile up on the floor, but these were placed or thrown there by the teenager. The bed might become unmade, but this was done by the teenager. Discarded papers might accumulate in the nooks and crannies of the room, but they were intentionally discarded by the teenager. The disordering of the room was not random. In fact, disorder really had nothing to do with it. You could not compare the room before and after and say which is more disordered because they are both ordered, just in different fashions. It is true that to someone who prefers things tidy the room will appear disordered, but to someone who does not mind a "mess," the room may appear organized at least in some sort of careless way.

Of course this example does not really describe entropy or the second law of thermodynamics; it is merely a convenient way for teachers to illustrate the concept at a beginner's level. Unfortunately, this gives students the wrong idea. Not only does it make students think of entropy as disorder, it also makes it seem like the second law of thermodynamics can be applied to macroscopic situations that have little or nothing to do with energy. Case in point, less than a year ago I was grappling with a different issue: life. "If entropy must always increase, how can life exist?" I wondered. Life seemed to me to be a much more ordered state than inanimate particulates. After much thought, I stumbled onto a solution that satisfied me: life can only exist because, though it is in itself order, it creates more disorder than non-living things could ever achieve. It seemed ingenious to me. Life's answer to the problem of entropy was entropy itself. I now realize that the concept of entropy does not really apply to this, especially since entropy does not actually have anything to do with disorder.

Let me explain what entropy really is, as I discovered recently while researching for this book. It is a measure of energy dispersal. Energy tends to disperse if not blocked from doing so. This is because atoms and molecules are in constant motion, and they continually bump into each other, transferring their energy. Picture a pool table with the balls all in motion. When they hit each other, they bounce off in different directions and with varying speeds as determined by the law of conservation of momentum. The same thing is happening on a much smaller scale all around us.

Think about the hot pan cooling in the air. The molecules in the pan are vibrating very quickly, which is otherwise known as heat. This is concentrated energy. The molecules in the air have more space to move in and are more spread out, meaning that they have less energy. When the air molecules knock into the pan molecules, they ricochet off, taking some of the energy from the pan's molecules. This means that the pan cools, and the air becomes slightly warmer. The energy disperses from a greater concentration to a lesser concentration, effectively averaging out. In terms of entropy, the state in which the pan is hot has low entropy, while the state in which the pan is cool has high entropy. Entropy has increased because energy has dispersed.

Entropy also increases when food dye is added to water. Picture it: you squeeze out a drop of blue food dye into a glass of water. Then you pull up a chair and watch. The concentrated color spreads throughout the water, slowly coloring the entirety of the liquid in the glass. The dispersal of the food dye seems random, but it is not. It is determined by the interactions between the food dye molecules and the water molecules. The water molecules are constantly in motion with a certain average energy. The molecules that make up the food dye are also moving with a certain average energy. When they enter the water, there is room to expand, so the molecules of the food dye and the water interact, colliding with other molecules and spreading out. Over time, the energy averages out as the solution reaches equilibrium. Entropy increases because the energy disperses, both from the food dye molecules to the water and from the water molecules to the food dye.

Evolution

As I mentioned earlier, evolution is based on random mutations. For anyone who doesn't fully understand the theory, I'll explain evolution briefly, starting with a definition of mutations. Mutations are deviations from the original DNA of an organism. Mutations in the germ line (or reproductive) DNA of organisms can be caused by a variety of DNA replication or reproductive issues or damage from external sources. These mutations are passed from parents to offspring. At times, the mutations can cause a change in phenotype, which is basically appearance or the physical results of the DNA code. If the mutations are favorable, more of the organisms will survive to produce their own offspring with the mutations as well. Over time, this causes changes that can lead to speciation.

For example, imagine a forest consisting of trees with dark-colored bark. There are a number of light-colored moths in the forest. A mutation results in a dark-colored moth. That moth survives because it is camouflaged from predators when it clings to a tree, and the moth reproduces. Some of the offspring are dark-colored, and more of the dark-colored moths survive and reproduce than the light-colored ones. Over time, the population of moths in the forest becomes predominately dark-colored.

Anyway, back to randomness. If nothing is random, what does this mean for evolution? The mutations essential for natural selection all have causes. The organisms that survive to reproduce were guaranteed to survive and reproduce. If this is the case, everything has led to the present. It might be tempting to see this as intelligent design. If all mutations led to the modern array of organisms, is this the result of some master plan? Not necessarily. Assuming non-randomness, evolution has led to the present state of organisms, and it also leads to the future present state of organisms. However, it does not lead to the present for any particular reason. There is no sign that all of this is done with forethought and planning. Evolution occurs because it has to occur. It is an observation of a natural tendency towards adaptation, though neither the individual organisms nor an all-powerful creator, as far as we know, has control over how the organisms adapt. Only the past controls the present.

Another tendency when considering non-randomness in evolution is to make the mistake of thinking that the purpose of evolution is to create *Homo sapiens sapiens*, or the current existence of humans. This is incorrect. The purpose of evolution is to create the present state of all organisms, although geneticists will not like the word 'purpose' to be used in conjunction with evolution. I think in this case they will understand my point. Think back to the cone web idea of causes and effects. The past has led to the present, but this cone will not converge at any future point. It will only further diverge, like the energy dispersal we discussed with entropy. Evolution creates an array of organisms, not a single point. For this reason, we as humans cannot think of ourselves as better than any other organism. We are not the triumph of evolution. We are merely one organism in a large array of organisms all fashioned through evolution.

The Computer Conceptualization

Let's do a thought experiment to see what's possible if nothing is random and there is no free will. Imagine that there was a very powerful computer, much more powerful than anything we currently have, and that you could program the computer with every existing condition in the Universe at this precise moment. The computer would be an exact replica of the Universe at a moment in time. Now press play and let time unfold in fast motion. Theoretically, the computer could reveal the future. Since the future is completely determined by the present and the past, a machine that took all of this into account should be able to calculate the future.

Here's the problem, though: if such a computer were built, it would have to take itself into account since the computer would also exist in the present. This creates a paradoxical situation. The only way the computer could function properly would be if someone locked themselves in with the machine and never came out. Then they could see what would happen in the future. However, if anyone let people know anything at all about the future, all kinds of problems would occur. The computer would already have taken this into account, most likely causing an error. The computer could not tell anyone the future if that person would then do something to change that future. The exception would be if the future depended on someone finding out a fake future and creating a real one the computer could already foresee.

Let's look at an example. Suppose the computer reveals that there is going to be a terrorist attack on a specific date. If someone is monitoring the computer, they learn all they can about how the terrorist attack happens in order to stop it. However, the computer knows that this is going to occur. How does this affect the future it shows? Can the future be changed by knowledge of what will happen in the future? Since the computer knows that people will try to change the future and how they will try to change it, it will either have to show a future that is constantly changing or one set future that cannot be changed.

I have to assume that the computer would show an unchangeable future or no future at all. This is because the computer would have already accounted for any interference from people who had seen the future it showed. The issue is that whoever is monitoring the computer should see the interference and how it does not change the outcome. Regardless, they must still try to interfere or else they would not have seen interference to begin with. This creates a loop that is difficult to understand. The important thing is that though seeing the future is theoretically possible, it probably wouldn't impact anything.

<u>So Why Bother?</u>

By now you may be asking yourself some depressing questions. If nothing is random and you have no free will, why bother anymore? Does anything you do even matter? The answer is actually yes. The reason is simple: everything you do affects the world. Even if you do not control your own actions, your actions still impact others. You are a variable in the equation of life. Nothing would be the same without you. The Universe needs your presence because you are a part of the Universe. Take comfort in that.

You should also take comfort in the fact that you can't change the past. Everything that happened in your life was going to happen and there was nothing you could do to change it. If you do something stupid, don't worry about it. You had no other option. You are supposed to be exactly where you are today, having gone through what you went through. So don't beat yourself up over a bad decision. You had to make that decision. Just move on with your life. The Universe will move on with you.

Made in the USA
Monee, IL
21 March 2025

14378585R00026